Dividend Stocks

How to Invest in Dividend
Stocks to Maximize Your
Return and Grow Your
Portfolio Whether the Market
Goes Up or Down

by David Berman

Copyright 2018 Beryl Assets LLC - All rights reserved worldwide.

Published simultaneously in Canada.

Disclaimer: This document is designed to provide accurate and authoritative information in regard to the subject matter covered. It is offered with the understanding that the presenters are not engaged in rendering legal, accounting, or other professional service. If legal advice or other expert advice is required, the services of a competent professional should be sought.

Adapted from a Declaration of Principles which was accepted and approved equally by a Committee of the American Bar Association and a Committee of Publishers and Associations.

The information provided herein is stated to be truthful and consistent, in that any liability, in terms of inattention or otherwise, by any usage or abuse of any policies, processes, or directions contained within is the solitary and utter responsibility of the recipient reader. This information has been obtained from sources believed to be reliable. The author made diligent efforts to ensure accuracy, however it is stressed that the information is provided with no guarantee (1) of accuracy, (2) of absence of error or (3) of absence of omission. You should always verify any and all information through your own sources.

Under no circumstances will any legal responsibility or blame be held against the publisher, the author or Beryl Assets LLC (hereafter and together the "presenters") for any reparation, damages, or monetary loss due to the information provided in this book, either directly or indirectly.

The information presented in this book represents only the opinion of the author as of the date of its publication.

Respective authors own all copyrights not held by the publisher.

The information herein is offered for general information purposes solely, and is universal as so. This book does not provide complete information on the subject matter and cannot, as such, be used as a sole source of information. The presentation of the information is without contract or any type of guarantee assurance. No information contained in this book constitutes investment, tax, legal, stock, equity or insurance advice. This book should not be considered either as communicating an invitation to engage in investment activities. You should determine your own investment decisions and strategies based on your own judgment and on your personal and specific financial circumstances. You should also keep in mind that investments can result in a loss and understand that you should always consult a competent professional before taking any investment decision and before putting any funds at risk.

LIMIT OF LIABILITY/DISCLAIMER OF WARRANTY: WHILE THE PUBLISHER AND AUTHOR HAVE USED THEIR BEST EFFORTS IN PREPARING THIS BOOK, THEY MAKE NO REPRESENTATIONS OR WARRANTIES WITH RESPECT TO THE ACCURACY OR COMPLETENESS OF THE CONTENTS OF THIS BOOK AND SPECIFICALLY DISCLAIM ANY IMPLIED WARRANTIES OF MERCHANTABILITY OR FITNESS FOR A PARTICULAR PURPOSE. NO WARRANTY MAY BE CREATED OR EXTENDED BY SALES REPRESENTATIVES OR WRITTEN SALES MATERIALS. THE ADVICE AND STRATEGIES CONTAINED HEREIN MAY NOT BE SUITABLE

FOR YOUR SITUATION. YOU SHOULD CONSULT WITH A PROFESSIONAL WHERE APPROPRIATE. NEITHER THE PUBLISHER NOR THE AUTHOR SHALL BE LIABLE FOR DAMAGES ARISING THEREFROM.

Any stocks mentioned in this book are for illustrative and educational purposes only. Under no circumstances does it imply that you should invest in these stocks nor that they could be appropriate for you. It's the reader's responsibility to conduct his own due diligence and to make his own decisions.

The trademarks that are used are without any consent, and the publication of the trademark is without permission or backing by the trademark owner. All trademarks and brands within this book are for clarifying purposes only and are owned by their respective owners. Beryl Assets LLC and the Author are not associated nor affiliated with any product, vendor or trademark owner mentioned in this book.

Companies mentioned are for example and illustrative purpose only. No company is endorsed or recommended. Just ideas, for you to decide if it's right for you after seeking the assistance of a competent and appropriate professional: lawyer, accountant, financial advisor, mortgage broker or else. The author, the publisher and Beryl Assets LLC do not provide any legal or other professional advice.

With respect to any third-party website or company mentioned in this book the reader is hereby prompted to read and acknowledge their respective terms and conditions before using them. The presenters assume no responsibility whatsoever in connection with their use.

All right reserved: No part of this book may be reproduced or utilized in any form or by any means, electronic or mechanical, including photocopying, recording or by any information storage and retrieval system, or distributed without permission in writing of Beryl Assets LLC. In no way is it legal to reproduce, duplicate, translate or transmit any part of this document in either electronic means or in printed format. Recording of this publication is strictly prohibited and any storage of this document is not allowed unless with written permission from the publisher. All rights reserved.

Table of Contents

Introduction	1
What are Dividend Stocks?	5
Dividend Basics	15
Dividend Terminology	23
Stock Dates Explained	31
Compounding	37
Dividend Reinvestment Plans	45
Comparison, Estimation, and Research Tools	53
Tools to Maximize Income	65
What are REITs?	73
Conclusion	83
Check Out My Other Books	87
Bonus	89

Introduction

Welcome to 'Dividend Stocks: how to invest in dividend stocks to maximize their return. The concept of this book was born out of the necessity to understand dividend-paying stocks and how to leverage your portfolio to maximize your income through smart investment strategies.

Dividend stock trading is a very simple process. It involves researching the market for the best dividend providers, assessing the risks in the companies you invest into and following the market to know when to sell off, buy more or compound the investment.

Smart dividend stock trading is a game of patience and is not a high yielding investment. This is a solid investment process for the long term and it is used to build up a solid portfolio.

This e-book will provide an insight into dividend stocks, their history, their dependence on the human factor and finally, ways and tools to trade to maximize your dividend stock portfolio. I will cover cash, stock, and property dividends. I will also take a look at what we call REITs and review ways of compounding. Finally, I explain to you the DRIP process. For now, all these acronyms may seem complicated and technical, but they will become apparent and easy to remember while reading this book.

This book has been designed for new investors and for non-professional investors looking to learn more about an investment instrument that they have heard about but do not really know. My goal, here, is to help you understand the basics of dividend stocks trading and why it can be a powerful investment strategy.

I am an investor with about 30 years of stock investment experience. Like you, I have been a beginner and as such I understand where you may be coming from. I understand the questions you may have and I will try to answer them all in the following chapters, always going to the point, and being the most concise I can be. Here, you will find no unrealistic promises of gains, no unverifiable claims, and of course – last but not least – you will not find the secret formula that will make you become a millionaire overnight. I leave that to the gurus! What I will do, instead, is much more valuable, and I hope you will agree much more serious: I will guide you through the basics and proven methods that any dividend stock investor should understand before putting any money at stake.

These foundations being laid, I hope you enjoy this book and I wish you the best.

What are Dividend Stocks?

Dividend stocks are stocks that pay out either cash or stock amount to shareholders and is dependent on a number of key factors. There are two main types of dividend stocks, those that pay out cash and those that pay out in shares. The term "dividend" means a sum of money that is distributed on a fixed term basis and paid according to a specific holding amount.

Cash Dividends

These are the more common forms of dividends founds, and the payout is directly related to the number of stocks a person owns. There are two kinds of cash dividends; these are preferred stock and ordinary shares. Preferred stock is given a set dividend payout value and holders enjoy these profits on a regular basis. Ordinary shares will have dividends decided upon by the board of directors. This is a discretionary process, and you will find that there are only three kinds of companies; those that give out dividends on a set term basis, those that give out dividends when profitable situations arise, and those that don't give out dividends at all (or mostly never).

Special One-Time Dividends

As mentioned above, some companies might decide to share in the company's profits through a one-time dividend payout. This is a rising instance since the tax on dividends is lower than on earned wages, many companies will utilize this method of dispensing cash without overburdening the receivers with tax. This means that employees, especially directors with a large holding in shares will enjoy a large bonus.

Another instance of a one-time dividend payout is when a company call the dividend a *"return of capital."* This means that the payout is not based on profits, but on the investor's investment to the company. These kinds of payouts are tax-free, and therefore not frequent.

Property Dividends

A less frequent dividend is a property dividend, where investors are given ownership of assets other than cash or shares in the stock. Dependent on the company's assets, property dividends can represent anything from pencil sharpeners to Manhattan skyscrapers. The property is evaluated, and this value is then attributed to the shareholder. In essence, if the asset is sold, then the shareholder will get their part of the income from the sale. In regard to investment property which makes a profit, most investors tend to retain them as a source of extra income rather than sell off.

Stock Dividends

Stock Dividends are pro-rata distribution of extra shares in the company's stock. It is usually given to holders of common stock. This dividend option is usually used when a company has no liquidity or when it wants to release more shares to increase tradability. The reason a company might reduce stock prices through a stock dividend is psychological and financial. Many investors will prefer to trade in $10 shares rather than in $10,000 shares. And as you can also imagine, some investors will not be able to buy expensive stocks, preferring to go for cheaper ones.

An Example of Stock Dividends:

The Company XYZ has 1 million shares of common stock. XYZ has five investors who each own 200,000 shares. The stock now trades at $100 per share, giving XYZ a market capitalization of $100 million.

The board of directors decides to issue a 20% stock dividend. It prints up an extra 200,000 shares of common stock (20% of 1 million) and distributes these to the shareholders based on their current holdings. All the investors own 200,000, which is one-fifth of XYZ, so they each receive 40,000 of the new shares (one-fifth of the 200,000 new shares issued).

XYZ has 1.2 million outstanding shares; each investor owns 240,000 shares of common stock. Stock prices fall to $83.33 due to the 20% dilution in the value of each share. However, XYZ and the investors are still in the same position they were before. Instead of owning 200,000 shares at $100, they now own 240,000 shares at $83.33. This means that XYZ's market capitalization is still $100 million.

What we have is a stock split that acts like a dividend, in which a company will increase the holdings per share by double to quadruple in number. The market will react in the way the company is expected to head, which means; if the company's split is due to liquidity issues, the shares might go down momentarily, if however, the split was to make the company more tradeable then the shares might react by going up in value.

There is a theory that the stock dividend option is a better one for investors. Any investor receiving extra shares will be able to decide whether to hold onto them or sell them at their own discretion. This will give them control over the amount of tax they pay per sale.

Summary

Dividends are a form of payment made to an investor or director that compensates them for the profitability of the company. You will find that most of the larger and more stable companies traded over stock exchanges will opt for giving dividends on an annual or bi-annual basis. This is partly due to the boards desire to receive extra cash from a lower tax bracket as well as making their shares highly tradeable since many corporate investors will prefer companies that make dividend payouts a regular form of return on investment (ROI).

Investors that seek a more stable long-term portfolio will always include a percentage of dividend stocks in their portfolio mix, and the larger the percentage of dividend stocks, the more stable the portfolio.

Dividend Basics

When a company generates profits, it can then distribute a percentage of these profits to its shareholders. Dividend payouts cost less in taxation and are a good source for a return on the investment (ROI). They are also a tool in the hands of the owners of privately-owned companies to funnel out money without paying high taxes on wages.

In general, part of the profit is set aside for liquid cash value, a percentage for research and development, a percentage for reinvestment and the rest can be distributed.

A lot of companies do not pay out dividends, those that do are split between those that do so on a frequent basis and those that are erratic. It happens that companies that are known for their dividend payouts decrease or even stop them completely. Among the biggest global companies, dividends are part of the corporate culture. Some companies have been paying out dividends for about 100 years, and have been annually increasing their dividend payout for decades.

Dividend Yield

This is the basic metric used to calculate a company's total ROI, which is a useful tool for checking out its potential in maintaining a good and sizeable number of shareholders.

Calculating a stock's dividend yield

The basic calculation is simple:

$$Dividend\ Yield = \frac{Annual\ dividend\ per\ share}{Price\ per\ share}$$

For example Company XYZ is trading at a value of $48 a share, and the board of directors decides to announce a dividend payout of $1.48 a share. This would give you a dividend yield of 3.08%. (1.48/48). Take into account that the price moves opposite to the yield, which means that the higher the stock value, the lower the yield and vice versa. The yield value of the payout is crucial to understanding the mechanics of company finances. The higher the yield percentage, the less viable the company's financial status. The reasons could be varied and many, one of the best reasons is that the board of directors is bleeding the company dry, which is the case in many private organizations. The basic key in this equation is the 100% cap. If the payout ratio is over 100%, this is a sign that the company is taking more money out that it is making in profit.

In general, the public stock market yields (S&P 500) tend to range between 1.17% and 3.23%.

Example

Here is a list of NASDAQ dividends, a partial one since the full list is 1,010 registered companies.

Symbol	Name	Last Sale	Annual dividend	Dividend yield	Ex-dividend date	Dividend Payment date
AAL	American Airlines Group Inc.	53.18	0.4	0.7479	2/5/2018	2/20/2018
AAON	AAON Inc.	35.4	0.26	0.7334	11/29/2017	12/21/2017
AAPL	Apple Inc.	176.21	2.52	1.44	2/9/2018	2/15/2018
AAXJ	iShares Trust	76.9	2.467588	3.221	12/19/2017	12/26/2017
ABAX	ABAXIS Inc.	68.64	0.64	0.9676	2/28/2018	3/15/2018
ABCB	Ameris Bancorp	54.05	0.4	0.7547	12/28/2017	1/10/2018
ABDC	Alcentra Capital Corp.	7.44	1	13.2802	12/28/2017	1/4/2018
ACET	Aceto Corporation	7.35	0.26	3.6984	12/15/2017	12/28/2017
ACNB	ACNB Corporation	28.25	0.8	2.852	2/28/2018	3/15/2018
ACT	AdvisorShares Trust	25.16	0.04477	0.1809	12/27/2017	12/29/2017
ACWI	iShares Trust	72.21	1.338726	1.8624	12/19/2017	12/26/2017
ACWX	iShares Trust	49.62	1.056	2.1355	12/19/2017	12/26/2017
ADES	Advanced Emissions Solutions Inc.	10.58	1	10.2775	2/20/2018	3/8/2018
ADI	Analog Devices Inc.	89.53	1.8	2.0383	11/30/2017	12/12/2017
ADP	Automatic Data Processing Inc.	113.6	2.52	2.2146	12/7/2017	1/1/2018

Remember the yield ratio, well on this table (dated March 5, 2018), you can start making your own opinion about what company can be viewed as more or less weak and which ones are showing strength in their numbers.

Keep in mind that this is simply an exercise for educational purposes. I picked these stocks completely randomly just for this exercise. This is in *no way* an investment recommendation or suggestion. I do not provide any such recommendation or suggestion.

Dividend Terminology

Since investment is a complex science, there is a whole stratum of terminology that is specific to the day to day discussion. Here are some of the most common terms used.

Cash Dividend

A cash payment made against the number of shares held in common or preferred stock. The exact amount paid is determined by the payout and the investor's holdings. The payout can be made for a number of reasons, the most common being current earnings or accumulated profit. The payout frequency varies per company.

Declaration Date

The date a dividend payout is announced or declared by a company's Board of Directors.

Dividend

The amount of distributed wealth that a company will assign for distribution amongst its shareholders. The value of the dividend divided by the number of shares determines the value per share each investor will receive.

Dividend Cover Ratio

This is the ratio between a company declared net dividend payout and the actual reported earnings. This ratio will show whether a company has sufficient funds to finance the payout. The actual calculation is Earnings per Share (EPS) divided by the Dividend Value per Share (DPS).

Dividend Reinvestment Plan DRIP

A DRIP (which we will discuss further in this book) is an opportunity for an investor to convert their cash dividend into a share dividend of equal value. This gives the company higher liquidity in both cash and shares and enables investors to increase their holdings without paying taxes.

Dividend Yield

The dividend yield is the method used to calculate the relation between a dividend payout and its share price.

$$Dividend\ Yield = \frac{Annual\ dividend\ per\ share}{Price\ per\ share}$$

Ex-Dividend Date

The ex-dividend date is the date that the stock trades without a dividend. This means, that if you purchase a share in a dividend yielding stock on or after the ex-dividend date, you will have to wait for the next payout date.

One-time Dividend

This is either a one-time special payout over normal dividend payouts or a one-time dividend payout in a company that does not usually give dividends.

Payment Date

This is the dividend payment date, it is declared ahead of time.

Record Date

This is the date used by a company to determine its shareholders or "holders of record" for dividend payouts purposes.

Shareholder (or Stockholder)

This is a person, company or institution that owns at least one share in a company.

Stock Dividend

These are dividends that payout in extra shares in the company. Either through a split or through a requested replacement of cash for stock.

Stock Dates Explained

While I covered dates in the terminology section, they are an important element to understand for any stock investor and require a more comprehensive description. Misunderstanding dates can have a direct financial impact on your return. There are four different dates that you need to understand.

The Declaration Date

The board of directors sets this declaration date. It is the date that the dividend is announced. The official statement will include the size or value of the dividend, the record date, and the payment date. The declaration date is a binding moment since, from the moment of the declaration to the payment date, the company must have the assets to fulfill the declaration.

The Record Date or Date of Record

Within the declaration date is the record date. This is the date that records the investors in the company. From this moment on, anyone registered as a shareholder will be found in the company records and will receive as "holders of record" all the relevant internal reports, financial and other relevant data that the company shares with its investors.

The Ex-Dividend Date or Ex-Date

The ex-dividend date is a cut-off date. From this moment you will not receive a dividend if you intend to invest. It means for instance that if the ex-dividend date is set for January 22nd and you intend to buy shares on the 23rd, even though the dividend payout will be the 30th of March, you cannot partake in the dividend.

The ex-dividend date is usually set a day before the record date.

This date is extremely important to follow if you intend to invest in dividend shares for their payout dates.

There are "dividend hoppers," investors that go in on a day before the ex-dividend date, just for the dividend payout and not to tie up their cash for too long. Take into account that dividend shares tend to fluctuate upwards towards the record date, and then to relax immediately after. This is due to the relaxation in trade since everyone is now waiting for the dividend payment date.

The Payment Date
Payable Date

The payment date is when the actual dividend payout in cash or stock is made. Only shareholders that invested in the stock before the ex-dividend date will enjoy the payout on the payment date.

Compounding

If you intend to invest in dividend stocks, then you should also learn a bit about compounding. This is the process by which you increase your direct profitability or your ROI from a specific dividend paying share. Due to the fact that dividend-paying companies tend to be financially stable and, in many cases, global companies, investing in them is usually a good idea - even without the dividend payouts. In most cases, these companies tend to increase in value over time, so there is a double profit made when investing in them.

Compounding in stock or cash dividends is actually quite common. A lot of investors seek out dividends to increase their holdings and their profits by investing in solid companies that have a proven track record of accomplishment for continuous growth. Such large global entities exist, and they provide a constant growth in stock value as well as a yearly dividend payout.

The general rule of thumb is that a constant dividend sharing company will likely continue to generate good ROI for its investors. Usually, these companies maintain a stable stock price and are healthier to invest in than companies that do not share their profits.

What is nice about dividend paying shares is the slow and solid performance they provide, day in and day out, for investors. Young people starting families should consider portioning part of their monthly income and buying up such stocks, compounding the payout into buying more stocks of the same company with every payout. After 30-40 years, these investments will provide an exceptional pensions cushion.

The Compounding Power

Albert Einstein called compounding the "eighth wonder of the world." He was not wrong. There is definitely something wonderful about compounding income.

Compounding means adding the interest of one value back into the original value and then recalculating the value to give a new interest figure. In reference to dividends, this means that the return on investment or dividend payout will be reinvested into the original stock, either through buying more stock with the dividend money or gaining more stock with a stock dividend payout.

Just to get a taste of compounding, in an exaggerated way, I am going to show you the compounded accumulation of doubling. This means we always double the number we have and continue to do so for 30 days. In this instance, we will start with 1 cent.

Day	Value	Day	Value	Day	Value
1	$0.01	11	$10.24	21	$10,485.76
2	$0.02	12	$20.48	22	$20,971.52
3	$0.04	13	$40.96	23	$41,943.04
4	$0.08	14	$81.92	24	$83,886.08
5	$0.16	15	$163.84	25	$167,772.16
6	$0.32	16	$327.68	26	$335,544.32
7	$0.64	17	$655.36	27	$671,088.64
8	$1.28	18	$1,310.72	28	$1,342,177.28
9	$2.56	19	$2,621.44	29	$2,684,354.56
10	$5.12	20	$5,242.88	30	$5,368,709.12

As you can see, the value of the initial investment for the first 10 days is relatively low, although in percentage the difference between 0.01 and 5.12 is exponentially large, and the final $5,368,709 should not come as a surprise. This example is not a natural occurrence since most dividend payouts will rage around the 1.5-2% mark, per annum. So, you can imagine what will happen over 30 years, and not thirty days. It will be an increase of 154% at a 2% increase per annum over 30 years. This might not seem a lot, but when you factor in the added savings the investor will place into the compounded portfolio, the overall profitability is very large and exceedingly solid.

Don't forget to add the stock price value which usually increases every year as well, the final value of the portfolio will actually be much higher.

Dividend Reinvestment Plans

Dividend reinvestment plans (DRIPs) are basically compound investment plans initiated by companies and investment firms to help investors automate the reinvestment of the cash dividend back into more shares of the same company. Dividend reinvestment plans work very well with companies that provide quarterly dividends. Usually, the company, or a transfer agent, and in many cases brokerage firms, provide the method for initiating a seamless dividend reinvestment plan.

One interesting feature of dividend reinvestment plans are the discount and commission-free fees that surround them. One way a company can keep its investors, as well as keep its profits is by persuading investors to reinvest the distributed wealth back into the company's stocks. Together with dividend reinvestment plans, some companies offer a discounted purchase of extra shares, between 1 to 10 percent, which will be added to the dividend reinvestment plans when it happens.

Companies that are frequent dividend distributors tend to prefer offering and managing the dividend reinvestment plans themselves. This means that the shares can be sold directly to the client, bypassing the stock exchange. This will free the proceeds from any handling charges that occur via the middle-people. Dividend reinvestment plans are a great vehicle for reducing company cash outflow and strengthening the ties between the company and its investors. Investors with long-term plans would prefer a dividend reinvestment plans scheme in any event since it increases their compounding potential. Dividend reinvestment plans are also useful for automating a system that sometimes goes through rough patches. Many investors with long-term portfolios will not be enticed to pull out unless they have financial problems that would warrant such an action.

From an investor's point of view, dividend reinvestment plans are the opposite of options, they are long-term systems for reinvestment of funds into stocks, and not quick in and out risks that speculators take. The actual enrollment into a dividend reinvestment plan is easy. It can be done online or in print and take a minute to fill out. Once the investor has initiated a dividend reinvestment plan, they can rest assured that their investment is now accumulating both stock face value as well as the stock amount. Since most schemes are either directly with companies or their representatives, there are little or no fees at all, and in many cases, the shares are bought at a discounted price. Extra shares can be bought for an even higher discounted price.

There is also the possibility of a split or partial dividend reinvestment plan where either some of the cash is taken out, or part of the extra stock is sold. This is done when there are usually large amounts involved, and taking out a percentage (such as 10%) can be used for other lucrative investments. When I say large, I mean over a million dollars' worth of stock.

Summary

Dividend reinvestment plans are an automated cumulative reinvestment system that enables investors to concentrate on other investment sectors that might need more focus. Dividend reinvestment plans will maintain a constant income from cumulative reinvestment of a dividend back into a share, thereby creating a scenario where dividends are paid over dividends saved.

Comparison, Estimation, and Research Tools

Due diligence is an important decision-making factor. This is true for dividend stocks as much as it is true for any investment consideration. Before you decide to buy the most lucrative looking share: compare. Make a list of companies that provide similar percentage payouts and look at all the companies' backgrounds, track records and media presence. Some companies might have a great past but a bleak future, while others might be solid investments that continue to expand on an annual basis.

Here are some of the basic tools for stock comparison:

1. Dividend Yield
2. Dividend Cover Ratio
3. Dividend Payout Ratio
4. History of Dividends.

Dividend Yield

As I discussed earlier, the dividend yield tells us how much a company pays in dividends each year in relation to the share price. As a rule of thumb, the higher the dividend, the riskier the investment. The lower the yield ratio means, the more stable the company.

$$Dividend\ Yield = \frac{Annual\ dividend\ per\ share}{Price\ per\ share}$$

However, other factors come into play, and this is not the only metric to use. To be effective, you need to check all the metrics, but also read up about the company and study its past performance as well as any pattern of financial management that could lead you to consider the investment too risky for a solid dividend source.

Dividend Cover Ratio

The Dividend Cover Ratio (DCR) is the ratio made between the earnings divided by its dividend payout. This ratio will allow you to estimate the company's liquidity to cover the dividend. This means that the lower the ratio, the higher the risk.

$$Dividend\ Cover = \frac{Earnings\ per\ share}{Dividend\ per\ share}$$

Example: Let's take two companies, A and B. A's earnings per share value is \$8.58 and will distribute a dividend of \$1.64 per share. The dividend cover for A is 5.23. B's earnings per share is \$5.91 but it intends to pay a dividend of \$3.36, which is a 1.76 cover. The rule of thumb here is that ratios between 2 and 3 provide adequate cover and the company is in a position to fulfill its obligations. Any ratio below 2 will show us a probable dividend cut in the future. If the ratio is below 1 it means that the company is using other sources of cash to cover the cost of the dividend, which is essentially saying, we are squeezing our cash cow dry. Any dividend cover that is over 3, or between 4 to 5 is a sign of a healthy company and has assets to continue its expansion.

Dividend Payout Ratio

This is the inverse of a dividend cover ratio. It shows us the percentage of earnings a company will distribute through its cash dividends. The dividend payout ratio (DPR) is calculated by dividing the dividend per share by the earnings per share.

$$Dividend\ Payout = \frac{Dividend\ per\ share}{Earnings\ per\ share}$$

Dividend payout ratio calculations are simple too. Let's take A and B again. With A the calculation of $1.64 / $8.58 gives us a DPR of 19%. The DPR of company B in comparison is $3.36 / $5.91 which gives us a 56% ratio. The lower the ratio, the more stable the company. So, in this instance, we see that A is a solid company and has ample assets to cover the payout, while B is going to have to dig deep to cover a payout that is over 50% of its earnings.

Dividend History

This is the crux of the matter. All the ratios will do is give you dry data that is easily understood but does not give you a real holistic picture. You need to dive deeper into the company's past and find the consistency of performance, investment in expansion and new markets as well as plans for a continuous supply of services or goods. All companies sit within a categorized division, food, aerospace, property, finance, biomedical, etc. Each category has different metrics and performances that would decide the nature of the company's exposure to risk and the possibility of stable to erratic income. By studying these facts, a bigger picture can be seen, and then the slight variances between dividends within sectors can be better understood.

Note that new dividends or companies that have not yet given out a dividend might decide it's time to do so, to attract new investors. These can be for a number of reasons, so check the company's history within their sector, compare a newly emerging company to an older one and consider the differences in variables. This means that some new emerging companies might have bright futures as new products hit the market, while older companies with strong backgrounds might not be developing a future marketing mix. The obvious candidates to compare are Nokia and Samsung.

Online Research Tools

There are many online tools to use for research purposes. These include business sites such as Bloomberg, which offers a comprehensive look behind the scenes. However, for proper research, nothing beats good old reading and comparing.

Start by selecting a number of dividend share companies that you wish to consider. Create an excel file chart, put in the name of the company, the dividend payout, the number of shares on the market and the current share price. Create four columns for the ratio calculations, and then arrange them in a

Pareto chart from the most solid to the riskiest.

Now go online and search historical data in Google, you just put in the name of the companies with the words stock price history. You will get an interactive chart to play around with. Check out the companies' prices for 10 years back. Now create an extra column and add the companies' stock value (total market value) now go into Forbes, and look for the companies Forbes ranking, if it is a big company.

The next step is to check out the company's dividend history, after which you look at their marketplace and then start to read up about any development plans for new products or services. I suggest you make a rating of one to five stars and make three columns, one for research and development investment, one for consistency of dividend payout and one for growth.

Now you have a basic decision-making tool that will tell you what the difference (delta) of risk between companies is. The next step is to research methods of investment that can maximize the potential of dividend payouts in a short time. This will be looked at in the next chapter.

Debt Restrictions

The final word on research, check the company's 10K SEC filings for debt restrictions that make limitations on distributing dividends. These are companies that you must be wary of and do not buy into them.

A Word about Taxes

I will not go into too much detail about dividend tax payouts since this is country specific and this book is intended for a global audience. I will just say that the taxes you pay on dividends you take out, are significantly lower than those you pay from wages or profit and gains taxes. Check your countries payout tax by entering into Google the following phrase "dividend payout taxes in (your country)."

Tools to Maximize Income

High Dividend Stocks

As with any successful portfolio management, working with dividend stocks is a science that requires skill and patience. More so patience since we are not discussing binary options or other fast-paced risky investments. Dividend stocks are all about the long game and waiting for the right moment, where the right moment might be three months away and the buy and sell time might be weeks rather than seconds.

If you want to become adept at mastering the arts of long-term lucrative dividend investment than you should start by identifying the shares that will payout and meet their obligations 100%. This entails knowing the market well, knowing which high paying stock payout will, and building a matrix of quick ins and outs as well as compounding more secure investments.

In a nutshell, maximizing your returns through dividend stocks is not going to make your percentages similar to investing in cryptocurrency markets, but it will give you a higher return year after year and will enable a compounded portfolio to deliver some impressive end of the year performances.

First of all, set a target, make a dividend mix based on a variety of companies. Use the long-term approach then choose your backbone for investment. The backbone company is a strong long-term survivor that has proven a constantly good track record and its future is set to provide the same over the next century. Now go to the market and look for high paying dividends from companies that have done so in the past and continue to do so. Use them as the second source of income, which you will compound back into your backbone account. The final step is to make sure you find all those one-off paying companies that offer a high return, but only occur once or twice in a decade. You will not lose your pants or your money when investing in a dividend stock, but you must be vigilant and must be aware of the risks of investment in general. In other words, companies are liable to change during periods of stress, and this will influence even the largest and most solid of companies. Payouts can be a problem if you enter a recession. So, just keep your eyes open on how markets can affect specific sectors of industry and trade.

Check out the cash flow of the company as well, sometimes GAAP net losses will show up with companies that offer a high payout dividend. Check out if this is a one-time affair and not an ongoing case. Usually, companies will not raise dividends if they are going through a continuous rough time. The same goes for companies that provide high dividends and do not lower them; this could be a sign that their difficult times are a momentary phase.

Finally: Rule of thumb, as Warren Buffet stated: "some of the biggest mistakes were made when relying on a reasonable supposition." Which means, don't take any situation for granted and question everything, even if it looks good and seems solid, check it out. After all, AIG was a great place once, and then along came subprime.

Summary

Unlike fast traded commodities, dividend stocks are a slow process that requires diligence and long-term research. While there are tools to maximize income, they all require the use of compounding and increasing holdings on a monthly basis. There are no real miracles here, just a lot of hard work and patience.

What are REITs?

A Real Estate Investment Trust, or REIT, is a company that specializes in owning investment properties that generate income. A REIT will source, buy, upgrade, maintain and market properties for solid income-seeking investors. Investors will buy a share in all of the real estate portfolio held by the REIT, or, in some cases, only a portion of a specific building. Properties can be office, commercial or residential, although some REITs might also invest in industrial and agriculture too.

In essence, REITs are a way to receive a dividend payout while investing in a solid asset. REITs originated around the 1960's and are similar to mutual funds. They offer investors the chance to own a portion of real estate and receive a dividend based on the income from the rents received.

Most REITs focus on specific sectors, such as healthcare, banking, warehouses, hotels, shopping malls, and condominiums. Some global REITs will have properties in many countries, and the management thereof will be dependent on local laws and tax regulations.

US-based REITs must qualify through:

- Invest a minimum of 75% of its total assets in either real estate, U.S. Treasuries, or cash.

- Earn at least 75% of its gross income from the real estate rents, mortgage interests, sales of real estate or through the financing of real property.

- They must distribute no less than 90% of all taxable income as dividends to the shareholders every year.

- They must be a registered corporation that is taxable.
- They must have a board of directors or trustees that manage the corporate strategy.
- There must be a minimum of 100 shareholders.
- No more than 50% of the shares can be held by five or fewer individuals.

Different REIT Categories

REIT's come in three forms, these are:

- **Equity REITs**

    An equity REIT will invest and own real estate properties that generate income for the shareholders and allow investors the chance to invest and share in the wealth. At least 90% of all the portfolio income must be distributed to the shareholders every year.

- **Mortgage REITs**

These companies invest in mortgages, they basically loan money to real estate owners and other REITs in the form of mortgages and special loan types as well as buying mortgage-backed securities. The income is from the net interest margin, and this makes such REITs sensitive to the fluctuations in interest rates.

- **Hybrid REITs**

Hybrids invest in various property mixes including mortgage based.

Investing in REITs

There are a number of ways to invest in a REIT. As a general rule, most REITs are private institutions and investing is done directly with them. Some advertise, others go by word of mouth. A few are also registered with the SEC or are public.

Before knocking on the door of a REIT, first, check out the property markets, and be specific. There are many sectors within the real estate industry, and each one performs differently, is open to different risks and provides different returns.

There are a lot of amateur REITs, companies that set up quickly to raise capital for immediate investment in a property. What you called term a "group buyout" where a group of individuals come together to buy a property and as such form their own pre-REIT group. After a while, the group buys more properties and grows. Usually, such groups start off like four or five individuals that target a property, they then try to persuade investors to invest in the property even before it is bought. After enough cash has been raised, the group will then buy the property, redevelop it if necessary, and start to distribute the wealth on a monthly or quarterly basis. They will promise phenomenal returns, but in reality, will sometimes not factor in the costs of maintenance and taxes. This will then be deducted, together with their 10% management fee. In many instances, investors are left with a percentage in a building that might make them 1-3% a year or even in debt due to maintenance fees.

Risks in REITs

Before you decide to invest in a Real Estate Investment Trust, make sure it is an actual REIT and that it owns properties. Make sure the company is registered, that it has a board of directors or trustees and that it has at least 100 shareholders. Also, check to see how much leverage their properties have. The best REITs own property without loans or mortgages. This means that they invest the shareholder's money in the real estate they buy without using bank loans. Loans and mortgages impact the profitability and reduce returns. While leverage is a useful tool to expand asset value, it can be a double-edged sword and as such, in a slow market, end up causing some properties to become burdens that eat up profits of the whole portfolio. Selling off the buildings can take time, and for quick sell-offs, the investment might end up becoming a loss.

Do not invest in companies or REITs that promise 15% ROI in unusual places, or even overseas. While there are countries where real estate is very cheap, the properties might have no income at all, or the investment in upgrading them would cost more than the purchase price of the original property. East Germany in the early years of the 21st Century was a classic example of such cases.

Conclusion

Dividends can provide a solid return on investment. They are generally considered secure by many investors since they usually come from secure long-term companies with solid backgrounds. But never forget that there is always a risk involved with buying financial instruments. Dividends can sometimes compensate the decline in stock prices but you can't bet on that and you have to realize that companies can live and disappear like individuals. Due diligence and monitoring are therefore very important.

When building a portfolio of dividend stocks, make sure you understand the mechanics of compounding, as well as of dividend hopping, where you buy in just before the ex-dividend date and sell the day after you get the cash.

For a long-term solution for an investment, it is best to mix your portfolio with a number of dividend stocks using a DRIP process. Let your money work for you in a passive way. Just remember to research your investment well before you invest and do not take anyone's words for granted. Even if the most capable investor or adviser advises you to invest in a specific share or REIT, check the details first.

If you have enjoyed this book, I would like to ask you if you would be kind enough to leave a review on Amazon. This may seem like nothing but it really does help to bring more great books.

Thank you and good luck.

Check Out My Other Books

Below you'll find some of my other books that are popular on Amazon and Kindle as well.

Penny Stocks: How to Invest and Trade Penny Stocks Like a Pro to Maximize Your Gains and Reduce Your Risks

Passive Income: Simple Ideas to Start Earning a Passive Income Today to Add Some Money in Your Bank Account or to Change Your Life

Look for these titles on Amazon!

Preview of
"Penny Stocks: How to Invest and Trade Penny Stocks Like a Pro to Maximize Your Gains and Reduce Your Risks"

What are Penny Stocks?

A penny stock is a company stock (or share) that has a value under $5 and that is usually traded over-the-counter (OTC) through the OTC Bulletin Board

(OTCBB) and pink sheets. On rare occasions, you will find some NYSE or other standard companies trading under $5 per stock. Unlike the main stock exchange traded penny stocks, most OTCBB traded penny stocks are highly volatile due to their low value and hard maneuverability including wide ranged bid-ask spreads and small capitalization.

As I stated, most penny stocks are limited to the OTCBB. Few companies can be traded on main exchanges, such as the Nasdaq, with share values under $5. This does not make those companies "penny stocks" in tradability only in name since their capitalization and tradability are high and fluid.

The big difference between a standard stock company and an OTC penny stock company is in the filing process.

OTC penny stock companies only require a market maker to support their request:

1. Either contact FINRA or OTC Markets Group Inc. and request to register for trade.
2. Provide a Market maker (Broker) that sponsors the request.
3. The market maker will Fill in form 211 on the FINRA or OTC MG site.
4. You are set for trade on the "Pink."

Standard stock companies are companies that make an initial public offering (IPO), which is the way all privately owned companies get traded on standard stock exchanges. An IPO is basically the process in which a company will try to raise funds to increase their credit and asset value to propel growth or to propel further research and development of a product before it gains access to a global market. All IPO's require specific preparations that include:

1. Forming an IPO team that includes an authorized underwriter, lawyers, Certified Public Accountants (CPA), and a Securities and Exchange Commission (SEC) expert.
2. The IPO team prepares a company profile with all the financials and

projections. This prospectus is then circulated for public scrutiny.

3. An official team of experts audits the financial statements.
4. Filing its prospectus and financial statements with the SEC and schedule the public offering date.

As you can see, there is a very big difference between how a regulated standard IPO is processed and how penny stocks are processed for trade. In general, penny stock companies represent companies that have limited access to private venture capital and that are seeking a de-regulated source of income that can provide them with large quantities of capital and a more fluid and public environment to work in.

While it is rare to find lucrative companies traded with penny stocks, it is not unheard of to find a few emerging technologies start from a simple penny stock company and transferring to the mainstream stock exchanges. There is also a reverse function too, where companies that were traded on main stock exchanges fell into debt or became untradeable and were transferred to trading on an OTCBB.

Other ways that penny stocks become standard stocks are:

1. The company can set up a new IPO with the SEC or a regulatory body
2. If a company reports that they have more than 2,000 investors.

3. If a company has more than 500 uncategorized (non-accredited) investors with an asset value of over $10 million.
4. If the company has listed its securities with a national security exchange such as the NYSE or NASDAQ.

In many cases, you will find that companies with over $10 million in assets would prefer a proper listing rather than a penny exchange due to the transparent nature and fluidity of trade. This means that most of the penny stocks are split between companies that are not worth the time to trade in and companies that are worthwhile investing in since they will emerge with a new technology or business model (such as with the gig economy) and require the IPO to raise the initial capital they could not get through private investors or financial institution loan channels.

• • •

Check out the rest of this book on Amazon.

www.ingramcontent.com/pod-product-compliance
Lightning Source LLC
Chambersburg PA
CBHW030950240526
45463CB00016B/2248